Marked States

Volume 2

On Feeling Good

Marked States Series Editor
Randolph Dible

randolphdible@gmail.com
https://randolphdible.com

On Feeling Good

An Operating Manual for the Human Consciousness

Being a discourse on the high states of consciousness in relation to the fourth, fifth, and sixth dimensions, with special reference to the possibility of inner development, the value of esoteric knowledge, and the nature of time and immortality.

Samuel Clarke McLaughlin

Originally published in 1978 by Autumn Press Inc

ISBN 978-1-84890-468-2

College Publications
Scientific Director: Dov Gabbay
Managing Director: Jane Spurr

http://www.collegepublications.co.uk

Illustrated by David Moberg
Cover produced by Laraine Welch

Table of Contents

Acknowledgements

My greatest debt and most pleasurable acknowledgment is to my wife, Constance, who has been teaching me about good feeling for thirty-five years.

Since the time of my first meeting with Walter Houston Clark in 1972, my increasing awareness of the significance of higher consciousness has been closely associated with the ripening of our friendship. By the example of his wisdom and integrity, and by the warmth and generosity of his person, he has conveyed to me his own fine vision of the possibility of infusing this society with the life and vigor of higher consciousness.

My good friend Bill Strovink has been a source of insight and information throughout the writing of this book. It was he who directed me, forcefully and repeatedly, to the writings of Peter Ouspensky; many of the themes that are developed in these chapters have their origins in Ouspensky's work.

Students at Tufts College, both graduate and undergraduate, were my daily companions during the years when this book was taking form in my mind: Cliff Shaw, who still listens patiently, comments with intelligence and wit, and shares generously his own knowledge and insight; Jon Earle, my principal source of information about research in states of consciousness; Bill Onifer, who did valuable library research for this book; Max Hirshkowitz, a serious student of higher consciousness; Ron McNutt, whose Altered States of Consciousness Organization has continued the tradition of higher consciousness on the Tufts campus; Dick Brown, Bill Onifer, Mary Jane Connaly, Jeanne Moran, Rick Phelps, Kathy Dudding, Barry Skoff, and many more.

My thanks also to my many friends among the faculty and administration of Tufts University. Seymour Simches, Frank Jones, Leonard Mead, Marian Perry, Eileen Howard, and many others all helped in various ways along the path that led to this book. I am particularly grateful to my farmer colleagues in the Department of Psychology, who made it possible for me to teach an unorthodox course—"Altered States of Consciousness"—as part of the regular curriculum, and who responded with patience and understanding as I gradually turned away from academic psychology.

A special word of appreciation to my friend and neighbor, David Moberg, for his illustrations; to my aunt, the Rev. Margaret

Jackson, who encourages me and keeps me thinking; to Sandy MacDonald, for editorial assistance; and to my publisher, Nahum Stiskin, who has a vision like mine and made this book from it.

Editor's Introduction

There is powerful magic in this text, and also in its title. The full original title of this work is:

On Feeling Good. An Operating Manual for the Human Consciousness. Being a discourse on the high states of consciousness in relation to the fourth, fifth, and sixth dimensions, with special reference to the possibility of inner development, the value of esoteric knowledge, and the nature of time and immortality.

The primary title of a book, like the proverbial "cover" we can't help but judge a book by, gives an implicit promise that it will not misrepresent the book's contents. This title—*On Feeling Good*—would seem to suggest that it is a self-help book. The secondary title's suggestion that it is a "manual"—*An Operating Manual for the Human Consciousness*—would seem to support that notion. In a certain way, it is a self-help book, but more so in the way that the works of Plato could be considered "self-help" books, than in the way that the works of the Stoics are. You can find multiple books on the Stoics at Target, but if you find Plato's *Republic* there it will not be because the target demographic is philosophical but only because the popularity of Stoic literature entails it. Certainly the ethical theory and practical advice of the Stoics have their roots in Aristotle's ideals of virtue and human flourishing, and the Stoics represent a rich metaphysical development of Neoplatonic philosophy all their own, including elaborate and technical cosmology and ontology, but too often today's popular interest in Stoic ideas drops speculative metaphysical thinking in favor of worldly empirical explanations and practical advice. This pop interest is nothing new. Sustained philosophical engagement with intellectual discourse about the mystical summoning of high states of consciousness, higher dimensions, esoteric knowledge and so on, have always been the themes of philosophers—that minority of the population inclined and able to dedicate their intellectual life to ideas.

"On the Good"

That this was also the case in Plato's day is attested by the reports about Plato's public lecture "On the Good" (τὴν περὶ τἀγαθοῦ ἀκρόασιν; Περὶ τἀγαθοῦ), and of the public disappointment it inspired. These reports—coming from Aristotle, Aristoxenus, Alexander of Aphrodisias, Albinus, Porphyry, Proclus, and others—relate that the topic drew crowds seeking to learn about wealth, health, and happiness, but were disappointed to hear Plato instead lecture about mathematics, astronomy, and the ultimate lesson that "the Good" is "the One." I contend that while this story about Plato's lecture offers a great way to approach McLaughlin's book *On Feeling Good*, McLaughlin is able to succeed with a popular audience where Plato wasn't in part because of an infusion of New Age ideas about universal love and compassion in the metaphysical Platonism and transcendentalism of psychedelic and self-help literature, and also in part because of the place of human emotional drama in the more speculative moments of today's science fiction imagination.

McLaughlin's contribution is needed today more than ever. It was an important expression when it first arrived in 1978, and it is even more relevant today, nearly a half-century later. The proliferation of possible worlds in the media of popular movies and science fiction series—both forms of popular literature in the inclusive sense: consider the quality of movies and shows with better or worse writing—regularly employ not only time travel and infinite time-loop scenarios but also alternate universes (mirror universes and possible worlds), often stemming from the realization of strange human interactions with the realities postulated by the scientific imagination of today's theoretical physics and cosmology, and also the depiction of psychedelic experience in extraordinary psychology. The strange physical circumstances surrounding quantum technology and such space-time anomalies as exotic matter and astrophysical holes in the ordinary space-time continuum are amplified and superseded by the emotional and valuational gymnastics that the merely partial immersion of the attention in such mediated imaginings make possible. Cosmic doses of psychedelic substances offer total immersion of human attention—fully and over-flowingly—in states of consciousness in which thoughts and feelings of higher-than-ordinary orders lead human operators to dramatically-other realms, and from there back to this one, often in such emotionally charged terms as one's life-mission, essence, and transcendental states of love and universal compassion.

Because the specific dimensionality of the space-time continuum within which we have our physical nature—and the broader continuum within which we have our fuller trans-physical nature, including, for instance, our thoughts and feelings—is only ever themified in physics and philosophy, the topic of dimensions is esoteric to the point of being quite intimidating. The title *On Feeling Good* is not intimidating. It is inviting, and promising. Most importantly, it makes good on its promise. While McLaughlin's mission is to convey a human and universal axiological vision consequent to an extraordinary ontology that is literally higher-order than the ordinary, just as Plato attempted, McLaughlin seems to succeed where Plato seems to have failed: with a popular audience.

On *Feeling* Good

On Feeling Good makes mystical esoteric philosophy understandable, like Huxley's *The Perennial Philosophy* (1945). It makes the dimensionality of space-time understandable, like Abbott's *Flatland* (1884). It distills the doctrine of higher dimensions found in the works of Gurdjieff and Ouspensky. Without making an explicit political statement, *On Feeling Good* implicitly makes a promise of hope to the political imagination, offering a way to universal humanity. In this way it is not unlike William Irwin Thompson's pamphlet *From Nation to Emanation: Planetary Culture and World Governance* (1982). Making good on these promises is something that occurred in the souls of the book's early readers, and in McLaughlin's students at Tufts University in the 1970s and 80s, but the demand for such making good has returned today.

On Feeling Good conveys its teachings to the reader's physical intuition, intellectual intuition, and emotional intuition. The nature of dimensionality is an ultra-simple lesson, and therefore it is also particularly susceptible to complication. To get past the feedback of thought and the redundancies of matter, one also needs the emotional or valuational aspect of extension—its feeling component—to become a theme. This is something McLaughlin achieves. Certainly Plato's erotic philosophy was more effective in this than the legend of his infamous lecture *On the Good* implies, but in any case we need this sense, this feeling, to come alive again today.

Dimension and Distinction

Dimensionality, general theory of extension, and the like, represent the planned but unconstructed cutting edge of today's latest developments within philosophy of the universal ontology of reality and of its inner- and outer-space cosmology and cartography. I call this part of the great edifice of scientific knowledge "unconstructed" despite the presence of a strong discourse regarding dimensions from mathematics and physics to psychology and philosophy of nature—from Euclidean Platonism to the nineteenth century advent of non-Euclidean geometries—because of the presently dominant aversion to otherworldliness within today's scientific attitude. Both higher and lower dimensions are extraordinary, and our understanding of these things needs to improve not only for their own sake but also for the sake of our naive understanding of the ordinary dimensionality of space-time. Of course there is spiritual scientific philosophy and there is the renaissance of the New Age, but materialism and mechanism remain powerful forces blocking access to the far side of speculation in the theoretical landscape of today. Hopefully our generation will witness a profound revolution in attitude.

On Feeling Good contributes a huge advance in the construction of both the foundation and the leading edge of human scientific culture because there are few other places to get such a detailed and accessible invitation to thinking about our higher-dimensional being. The thought experiments in this book present illuminating narrative explanations, in addition to the more widely available analytical explanations of higher dimensions. We will need to be able to imagine higher dimensions as well as develop a general theory of dimensionality if we are to advance intellectually to our next frontiers. We constantly re-enter our familiar continuum, but so much more is possible.

In *Process and Reality*, Alfred North Whitehead lays out his own answer to post-Euclidean crisis of geometry with a dynamical, process-based theory of extension. But his position also admits that the only constant is change, and novelty is the only sure thing, especially in such generalities as those addressed by metaphysics. "A precise language must await a completed metaphysical knowledge" (12), and this is especially the case with metaphysical knowledge of dimensionality and the linguistic tools of its expression. McLaughlin's book, especially the simple imagery of a *raindrop* developed through chapters 4 and 5, accelerates our linguistic and intellectual capacity for understanding dimensionality.

The Marked States book series, of which this second edition of *On Feeling Good* is a part, shares the aim of developing that unconstructed part of the plan of universal human knowledge. The 1969 publication of George Spencer-Brown's mathematical book *Laws of Form* introduces the distinction between the marked state (which is anything and everything) and the unmarked state (absolute nothingness; the absolute infinite; the beyond being) as the "first distinction." Like McLaughlin's perennial raindrop, this one simple entity is an Archimedean fulcrum for a paradigmatic revolution. The first extension of the first distinction is the first dimension. Distinction and dimension go hand in hand.

As a rethinking of Euclid's point, which the whole geometrical and dimensional series depends upon, such innovations of metaphysical language and thinking as these illuminate not only their proximate network of ideas but also represent new paths to a general universal theory. Whitehead writes "So far as mere extensiveness is concerned, space might as well have three hundred and thirty-three dimensions, instead of the modest three dimensions of our present epoch" (289). No matter the number of dimensions, no matter the state of things, true knowledge stands in true *universality*, and such universality is extra-ordinary, super-ordinary, or more precisely "*All*-ordinary:" it essentially includes all possible universes within its comprehension. McLaughlin's idea of the six-dimensional figure of the raindrop, and his cumulative and progressive narrative illustration of its nature, represents a *saltus inter ordines* in the meaning of universality.

The Portal Opes

Like both Whitehead and Plato, Samuel McLaughlin employs simple mathematics to re-align our intuitions of physical and psychical being with the absolute goodness that is the ultimate reality beyond all possible being. But Mclaughlin doesn't *feel* like an Athenian or Cambridge philosopher. McLaughlin's style, like his book's title, is inviting. Anyone can pick it up.

Today's psychedelic renaissance has paved the way for a return of the original spirit of psychedelia. This spirit returns in the vehicle of therapy—offering a path to homeostasis and functional behavior—but as spirit it is wild and primordial and will settle neither in a static holding pattern nor in mere reports or echoes of real and tremendous power that people experienced fifty years ago. Spirit is at once ancient and perennial, and future-oriented. The psychology of extraordinary experience and the philosophy of transcendence have their original roots in the spiritual teaching that bridges our world with ultimate reality, penultimate reality, antepenultimate reality, and the levels of being whose echoes are still audible in our ideas of number and geometry.

In light of the present return to the scientific use of psychedelics as a tool for the exploration of inner space and for the development of the proverbial "cutting edge," we might point to the latest innovation in the field of consciousness research of the use of DMT and DMTx as what Andrew Gallimore calls a "reality-switch technology" (2022). The opening of a trans-dimensional portal and the empirical experience of human subjects crossing through the gateway between the ordinary space-time continuum to an extraordinary continuum brings the wormhole of theoretical physics to the human physical and psychical reality, and to earth. Such technologies of the soul as John Lilly's flotation tank, and the phenomenological and ontological exploration and development connected to it, and the current work being done with DMTx, should bring into their fold McLaughlin's contributions, both from this book and whatever can be recalled of his old Altered States of Consciousness Society at Tufts University. The true human scientific spirit as well as the spirit which animates us coalesce in this work, and we need their cooperation now more than ever.

Randolph Dible, July 2024

References

Abbott, Edwin. 1992 (1884). *Flatland: A Romance of Many Dimensions*. New York: Dover.

Cooper, John M. 1997. *Plato: The Complete Works*. Indianapolis: Hackett.

Gaiser, Konrad. 2004. "Plato's Enigmatic Lecture 'On the Good' (1980)." In *Gesammelte Schriften*, ed. Thomas A. Szlezák. Sankt Augustin, DE: Academia Verlag.

Gallimore, Andrew. 2022. *Reality Switch Technologies. Psychedelics as Tools for the Discovery and Exploration of New Worlds*. Tokyo: Strange Worlds Press.

Huxley, Aldous. 2004 (1945). *The Perennial Philosophy*. New York: Harper.

Ouspensky, Pyotr. 1997 (1931). *A New Model of the Universe: Principles of the Psychological Method in its Application to Problems of Science, Religion, and Art*. Mineola, NY: Dover.

—. 1987 (1965). *In Search of the Miraculous. Fragments of an Unknown Teaching*. New York: Arkana.

Schilpp, Paul A., ed. 1941. *The Philosophy of Alfred North Whitehead*. Evanston, IL: Northwestern University Press.

Spencer-Brown, George. 2011 (1969). *Laws of Form*. Leipzig: Bohmeier Verlag

Thompson, William I. 1982. *From Nation to Emanation: Planetary Culture and World Governance*. Findhorn, Moray, Scotland: Findhorn Publications.

Whitehead, Alfred N. 1978 (1929). *Process and Reality: An Essay in Cosmology*. New York: Macmillan.

Preface by Ron McNutt

Sam McLaughlin was my teacher and my friend. He taught the most exciting class I ever took. During my sophomore year at Tufts in the spring of 1976, he taught Psychology 10, Altered States of Consciousness. The class brought over a hundred students to Goddard Chapel to hear inspiring and fascinating lectures by Sam and his invited guests, luminaries in the field of consciousness, on topics involving consciousness, dream states, meditation, Kundalini awakening, and religious use of psychedelic plant medicines, and LSD, and marijuana. Sam encouraged us to try to increase our understanding and to be open to the central experience of identity, awareness, experience. He wanted us all to notice and appreciate the many levels of consciousness and perception including the unconscious mind and its mysterious activity. A recurring focus of our lectures was the mystical experience and how the experience awakened the impression that the ego is less real than we usually believe, or less separate from the outer world, and the appreciation that there is an enduring awareness of the continuity of life.

Sam was unassuming and yet confident; he beamed with energy. He had done experiments in the Harvard labs of behavioral psychologist B. F. Skinner. He had a wide range of experience in psychology. He had researched natural ways to train children to overcome strabismus. At Tufts, he worked with a graduate student, Cliff Shaw, on computers looking into artificial intelligence. Sam had decided to retire early in his career and move with his wife Connie to their 1815 farmhouse in South Parsonsfield, Maine, with thirty acres of surrounding woods, through which he maintained pathways which led down to a beaver pond. Sam's refreshing openness to the potentials of psychedelics and marijuana were exciting to the students. Sam inspired me to form a student organization bearing the same name, and we formed a friendship that lasted until his passing in summer 2020.

After he retired, I was privileged to visit him and Connie. Occasionally, Sam and I would climb Mount Chocorua. He enthusiastically developed and expanded his interest in the dimensionality of human experience and discussing dimensions. Sam's interest was inspired by P.D. Ouspensky originally. He shared his insights with students as a guest speaker, discussing dimensions. He had an article published in a scholarly journal about dimensionality. Sam was very grounded in his retirement in the small town of South Parsonsfield, Maine. He explored ideas about dimensions and other creative thoughts while engaging in practical and strenuous work like shoring up the foundation of his old barn which he had converted to a garage. He had a nice garden with pathways, and he enjoyed the company of neighbors.

Ron McNutt, July 2024

Preface by Suki Dejong-McLaughlin

I can't thank Randy enough for making possible this second edition of my dad's book, *On Feeling Good*, originally published in 1978.

    I think the world is hungry for more scientific explanations like this on spiritual awakening; for what is actually happening outside our limited three-dimensional existence. The fourth-dimensional time window, as explained herein, allows the perception of time to be seen all at once through the illustration of looking out a train window while traveling as we watch the various scenes go by. By thinking of this as a time window, we can perhaps visualize the moment before the present moment, the present moment, and the future moment. Time is the fourth dimension, and deserves our rapt attention. Rest in power, Dad. I love you.

Suki Dejong-McLaughlin, July 2024

Introduction

I shall try in this book to say something straightforward and useful about the problem of bringing good feeling into our lives. If some of the topics dealt with here seem remote from that simple theme, it is because we have tasted the fruit of the tree of knowledge, and the simple route to good feeling—the path of blissful ignorance—is no longer open to us. To live with grace in the complex world we have created, we must achieve a degree of self-knowledge commensurate with our knowledge of how to destroy.

I shall show in this book that the physical universe has more than five dimensions, and that its apparent dimensionality is determined not by any property of the universe itself but by the state of consciousness of the observer. I shall then show that the higher levels of human consciousness (defined as the states of mind associated with good feeling) represent direct awareness of higher physical dimensions than those which we ordinarily experience. The psychological characteristics of the highest states of consciousness including direct awareness of the unity of all things and the consequent emotions of universal love and compassion are derived from the physical properties of the fourth, fifth and sixth dimensions. Thus, the human significance of the higher dimensions of the physical universe is that they represent and embody the transcendent element in human experience.

In short, whereas the lower dimensions constitute what we sense as "matter," the higher dimensions are (for us) "spirit." A proper understanding of the scale of physical dimensions therefore enables us to examine the relationship between those two broad categories of human experience, and to see them as differing in degree rather than in kind.

The principle I shall use in interpreting these observations is the principle of dimensional levels. The mathematical expression of this principle is that the relation between successive dimensions (between point and line, line and surface, surface and solid, and so on) is that of zero to infinity. The physical (material) expression of this same principle is that higher dimensional levels are superior to lower dimensional levels with respect to energy, informational capacity and content, and anything else that can be measured.

The principle of dimensional levels describes the single most fundamental property of the universe—a law as simple and reliable (and as obvious, once it is grasped) as the law of the lever. Moreover, this principle extends far beyond the universe that we know as "physical." It includes everything in human experience that is most worth seeking. Everything there is to know about the universe, and about ourselves in it, is merely a filling in of details between the broad strokes of the dimensional picture. The concept of dimensional levels of consciousness reaches from the *Sanctus* of the B-minor mass to the red-shift of the retreating galaxies.

The power of the concept of dimensional levels is well illustrated by the way it enables us to deal with the idea of "reality." In our ordinary usage, "reality" is an absolute term and designates a property of the "real world"—i.e., the "material" world as revealed to us by our senses. But when we take into account the fact that the universe (and we in it) are many-dimensioned, then it becomes clear that "reality" is a relative term, designating a property of higher dimensional levels. For example, if we try to conceive a two-dimensional surface existing within a three-dimensional solid, we find that the surface does not occupy any of the "space" of the solid, and therefore can only be an imaginary concept—cannot have any real existence—within the solid. Thus, the solid is "more real" than the surface, and, in general, higher dimensional levels are more real than lower dimensional levels. The same line of reasoning applies to such terms as "truth," "validity," and "veridicality."

The interpretation of the concept of dimensional levels of consciousness in terms of the physical principle of dimensional levels provides rational support for esoteric and religious teachings that have been advanced since ancient times as the fruits of intuitive wisdom. This interpretation confirms, for example, that the high states of consciousness are the most desirable of all human conditions and represent a transformation of the human psyche; and that the most commonplace of spiritual values infinitely exceeds the greatest conceivable material gain.

The application of the principle of dimensional levels enables us to approach with our intellect the reality that lies behind the illusions of space, time, and matter. With this system of ideas, we can bridge the gap between matter and spirit, between intellect and intuition, that is so deep a wound in the individual human psyche and in the body of our civilization.

There is little in this book that is novel or original. For the most part, I have simply restated some ancient truths in the modern idiom—i.e., in the language of rational inquiry. But I have also tried to keep in mind the advice of Francis Bacon, to "make the time to come the disciple of the time past, and not its servant." The ancient doctrines change in both form and substance when they are stated in terms of dimensional levels rather than in terms of gods and angels. New light is thrown on old enigmas, and obscure aspects of the teaching receive new emphasis. My hope is that this reformation will show more clearly the relevance of time-honored doctrines to our present situation.

There is also very little in this book that the reader does not already know. Education of the highest order, as Plato pointed out, is recollection. All the wisdom of eternity and infinity is lodged within us and is available to us from within. Many people believe that an understanding of the higher dimensions of the physical universe requires training in mathematics and physics. This is not the case. Anyone can understand the fundamental properties of dimensions. Like all unfamiliar concepts, they may require an initial investment of careful and thoughtful reading; but, once grasped, they are seen to be simple and obvious, and their presence can be sensed in the objects and events of ordinary experience.

We all have an intuitive understanding of dimensions, and we need only some terminology, and a plan or organization for the topic, in order for this knowledge to become conscious. The properties of the six dimensions of the universe, and the relation of these dimensions to human consciousness, are the fundamental facts of our existence and should be taught to every child in elementary school.

Chapter 1

If the day and night are such that you greet them with joy, and life emits a fragrance like flowers and sweet-scented herbs, is more elastic, more starry, more immortal—that is your success.

—Henry David Thoreau,
Walden

Man has become so earthly and outward that he seeks afar, beyond the starry sky, in the higher eternity, what is quite near him, within the inner center of his soul.

—J. G. Gichtel,
Theosophia Practice

Spiritual evolution can only be conscious. It is only degeneration which can proceed unconsciously in men.

—Peter Ouspensky,
New Model

Good Feeling and the Path of Knowledge

But what if man had eyes to see the true beauty—the divine beauty, I mean, pure and clear and unalloyed, not clogged with the pollutions of mortality and all the colors and vanities of human life—thither looking, and holding converse with the true beauty simple and divine? ... Would that be an ignoble life?

—Plato,
Symposium[1]

Good feeling doesn't always accompany success and physical comfort, but it often shows up as the unexpected companion of privation and exertion. It tends to elude us when we seek it directly, and then to appear unannounced when we have turned our attention to other things. Good feeling results from living life as it comes, and as it comes, it includes work and sacrifice, unrequited love and vain striving, sweat and toil and uncertainty, failure as well as success.

The reason why genuine good feeling is associated with life fully lived, rather than with the sheltered life of ease and luxury, is that it occurs as the outward manifestation of an inner creative process—a process in which we use the varied events of a lifetime to create within ourselves a being of higher order and higher dimensionality than the being we now are. This kind of good feeling can therefore endure hardship and suffering, and, indeed, be strengthened by them.

Any psychological condition or state of mind may be thought of as a condition or state of consciousness. The states of consciousness that are associated with good feeling are the high states of consciousness. These are the states of mind in which everything seems right, in which the body and the senses produce pleasant sensations, in which familiar things appear more beautiful and satisfying than ordinarily—colors brighter, sounds more pleasing, music more melodic and moving.

It is usually not difficult to attain a temporary condition of higher consciousness—we each have our own favorite methods. We may get "high" from social activities, from the ingestion of certain

---

[1] *Plato Selections*, ed. Raphael Demos (Scribner's, 1927), p. 268. These words are spoken by Socrates, quoting Diotima.

substances, from material success, or from being outdoors on a beautiful day. The challenge lies in attaining a stable condition of higher consciousness—a condition in which the base line of consciousness is raised to a new level, and in which we rise from that base line to higher levels than we had previously imagined to be possible.

From ancient times down to the present, a wide variety of methods have been proposed for attaining a stable condition of higher consciousness: religious devotion, meditative practices, the ingestion of sacred substances, specialized disciplines of breath control and mental concentration, and many more. Each has its special virtues, but fundamental to them all is one universal and indispensable method: the acquisition of knowledge about higher consciousness. This method is sometimes referred to as *jnana yoga*, the yoga (that is, method or path) of knowledge.[2]

Knowledge about higher consciousness works in several ways to raise the level of consciousness. For one thing, it is good news— namely, the news that the higher levels of consciousness can be attained by ordinary people. This book is intended as a statement of that news in such a way as to be encouraging and enlightening to those who are already familiar with the concept of higher consciousness, and persuasive to those who are skeptical.

A second way in which knowledge acts to raise consciousness is by making the high states more familiar. In matters of the mind, "knowing" is not entirely separate from "having," and states of mind with which we are familiar are always more accessible than those of which we have no knowledge.

The attainment of higher consciousness may also be thought of as a question of the intelligent management of one's inner self, and it is obviously desirable to approach such a task with knowledge and understanding rather than in ignorance. The yoga of knowledge is the fundamental and universal method in that it provides a rational basis for choosing among other methods, and enables us to use other methods effectively and safely, with an understanding of their rationale and with a clear view of the goal to be attained.

A more subtle advantage of the path of knowledge has to do with the fact that our state of mind is always strongly influenced by our knowledge of what to expect, and this is especially true of the high states of mind. By acquiring the concepts and metaphors which other people have derived from their own experience of the high states, we enrich and enlarge our own experience of those states. Without this kind of guidance, the high states can be nothing more than recreational

---

[2] For a historical treatment of jnana yoga, see Ernest Wood, *Great Systems of Yoga* (Citadel Press, 1966), pp. 61 ff.

8

episodes, soon forgotten; with it, they can become states of profound insight, unforgettable imagery, and strong intellectual content.

One of the most widespread misconceptions about the high states of consciousness is that one needs only some specific method, such as meditation or a psychedelic substance, to attain them. The paradoxical fact is that it is perfectly possible to be *in* a high state of consciousness without having the *experience* of higher consciousness. This situation, which is extremely common, arises when an individual uses one or another technique to achieve the physiological condition corresponding to higher consciousness, but without adequate preparation or guidance, and hence with no knowledge of what to expect or how to interpret the psychological changes that occur. It is impossible to *have* any experience unless one first has a frame of reference in which to fit it, a handle with which to grasp it and hold onto it. Otherwise, the experience can, so to speak, pass through one's mind without one's being aware of its full meaning. This property of the mind is not always apparent from our ordinary experience, but becomes highly significant when we begin to deal with the more extreme and unusual states of consciousness. We all live closer than we think to higher consciousness. The element we most often lack is knowledge of what to expect in such states and what interpretation to place on them.

The high states of consciousness are themselves sources of intuitive knowledge, but the knowledge they make available to us is always ambiguous, since it always contains both positive and negative elements and is difficult to grasp (and therefore to remember) with our logic-oriented minds. Knowledge that relates the experiences of higher consciousness to our every-day experiences, to things we already know and accept, can help us in our efforts to interpret and apply the intuitive insights that originate in the higher states.

The yoga of knowledge is also the method most compatible with the rational mode of thought with which Westerners approach the attainment of higher consciousness, and it is therefore a method of which members of this culture might be expected to show a special aptitude. It enables us to see the high states not as an irrational or unscientific or solely religious subject matter, but as a suitable object for rational inquiry, and as a type of human experience that has great significance for the individual and for human culture.

It is for these reasons that this book, which is intended as a practical guide for anyone wishing to attain a higher level of consciousness, contains little information about specialized faith and immortality, because a knowledge of these topics conveys the understanding on which special techniques are based. Such knowledge also has its own intrinsic value and interest. It is knowledge about an important and little-understood area of human experience, and about topics that are seldom discussed in rational terms.

It is not my intention, in emphasizing the method of knowledge, to imply that the more specialized techniques are not of great value when used properly. If this book should lead any reader to investigate and pursue the various methods for attaining higher consciousness, and to do so with a clear understanding of the nature of the goal and the hazards of the path, it will have served a useful purpose.

Throughout this book, whenever I refer to the attainment of a higher level of consciousness, I have in mind not the achievement of a specific level, but rather an opening up to the process which is manifested in spontaneous and unstudied acts of love and kindness, for such acts contain a higher wisdom, a fuller and more accurate symbolization of higher consciousness, than can be embodied in any "scale" of consciousness.

Chapter 2

Esoteric Knowledge

He who knows Brahma becomes Brahma.
—Mundaka Upanishad[3]

"Esoteric" suggests secret information, the jealously guarded property of a small group. But serious esoteric tradition places little reliance on secrets. Esoteric material is often difficult of access, but no more so than other forms of specialized knowledge. In the words of John Michell, "Although it is known as the secret or Hermetic tradition, its material content has never been hidden from anyone who felt inclined to study it."[4]

The real difficulty is not in gaining access to esoteric material, but in knowing how to interpret it. An esoteric text always has at least two levels of meaning: an exoteric level, which is the literal meaning of the words; and one or more esoteric levels, which are subtler and more obscure. There are many examples of such texts. Perhaps the most widely available is the text consisting of the first four books of the Christian New Testament.

Even the subtlety of meaning that characterizes esoteric material stems not from any attempt at concealment, but from an effort to convey truths that do not lend themselves to direct verbal expression—truths that are more adequately expressed in subtle metaphors, in the symbolism of numbers and geometric constructions, or in artistic and architectural forms. The purpose of esoteric material is not to hide the truth, but to preserve and transmit it.

Esoteric writings are extremely diverse, covering the entire range of human experience, but they are linked by several common elements. For example, most esoteric writings ascribe to numbers a significance that goes far beyond mere quantification. "One" is the monad, the One, the All, the unity of the higher reality. "Two" represents the duality of the material level of existence—the yin and yang of oriental religions. "Three," which appears as the triune divinity of many religious systems, is the combination of unity and duality, and represents the interaction between the two levels, out of which is created the universe of human experience. "The number," says R. A.

---

[3] *The Upanishads: Breath of the Eternal*, trans. Swami Prabhavananda and Frederick Manchester (Mentor, 1957), p. 48.

[4] John Mitchell, *City of Revelation* (Ballantine, 1973), p 16.

Schwaller de Lubicz, "thus represents the extreme reduction of philosophic thought."[5]

Numbers also provide a concise way of referring to a "sacred geometry," which is itself a complex area of study. "Five," for example, is the number of the senses and of humanity: it is represented geometrically by the pentagon or by the five-pointed star (pentacle or pentagram), as in the famous drawing by Leonardo da Vinci. "Six" is the number of the physical creation, the cosmos. The corresponding symbol, the six-pointed star (best known in our culture as the Judaic symbol), is sometimes used to represent the six dimensions of the universe. It is then shown as two interlocking triangles which refer, respectively, to the three dimensions of space and three higher dimensions. The complexity of meaning that resides in such a symbol will become apparent as we develop (during the next few chapters) the dimensional concepts that it embodies.

By such numbers and the implied symbols, a text such as the Gospel According to John is given subtle layers of meaning and is related to other texts which might otherwise be thought to derive from entirely unrelated sources.

Whether the topic is sacred geometry, esoteric physiology, Egyptology, or ethical philosophy, however, all esoteric writings have a common theme, a single truth which is enlarged and enriched by its many diverse expressions. It is the theme of this book: the doctrine that there are higher levels of consciousness to which human beings may aspire, and that those higher levels are infinitely more desirable than our present condition. This is the fundamental esoteric teaching, the one element that is common to hermetic and alchemical writings, the *Bhagavad Gita,* the enigmatic parables of Jesus, *The Teachings of the Compassionate Buddha, The Secret of the Golden Flower,* Plato's *Republic,* the *Enneads* of Plotinus, the *Upanishads,* and innumerable other sacred and secular texts.

The work toward higher consciousness always involves two complementary processes: first, the discovery that the goal—the higher level of consciousness—exists and is attainable; second, the actual attainment of the goal. The two are complementary, in that each leads into the other. Knowledge of a higher level makes possible its attainment, and the attainment of a higher level carries with it the awareness of still higher levels, thus starting another upward turn of the spiral. These two processes are the yin and yang of conscious evolution, the two legs on which any human being may walk the path of inner

---

[5] R. A. Schwaller de Lubic, *The Temple in Man*, trans R. and D. Lawlor (Autumn Press, 1977), p. 67.

development.

Two parables from the Gospel According to Matthew[6] illustrate these two states in the process. The first parable tells of "treasure hidden in a field, which a man found and covered up; then in his joy he goes and sells all that he has and buys that field." The second parable is the story of "a merchant in search of fine pearls, who, on finding one pearl of great value, went and sold all that he had and bought it." In each of these parables, the initial discovery—the first stage—is followed by a second stage in which personal sacrifices are made, and former beliefs and attachments abandoned, in order to realize this new possibility.

It is not always easy to distinguish between these two stages, because both are essentially stages of learning and growth. The distinction is especially difficult when, as in this book, one approaches higher consciousness by way of the path of knowledge, because then both stages (and not merely the initial discovery) involve the acquisition of knowledge. But for this very reason it is important to keep in mind the distinction between the two stages, because it reminds us that a balance is needed. It is all too easy to become lost in the intellectual pleasures of learning *about* the high states of consciousness and neglect the personal involvement and commitment that are needed to attain them; it is equally tempting to get bogged down in technique and forget the purpose of the technique.

---

[6] Matt. 13:14-66.

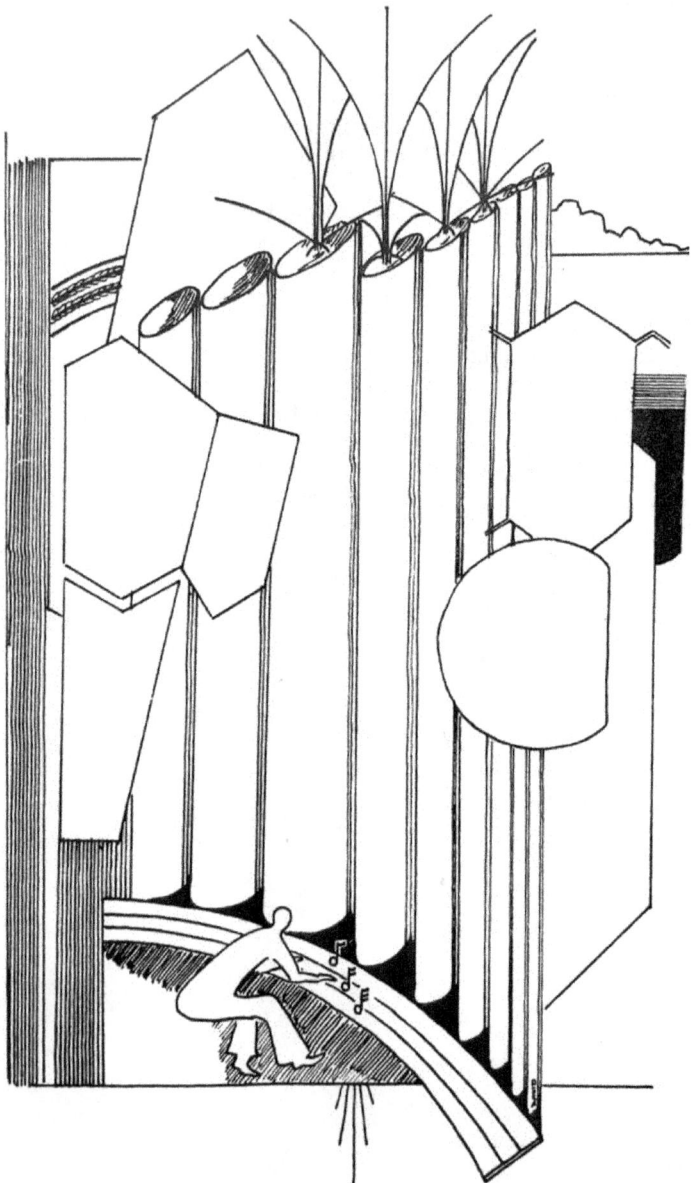

Chapter 3

The Highest States of Consciousness

The most beautiful and profound emotion we can
experience is the sensation of the mystical. It is the
sower of all true science. He to whom this emotion is
a stranger, who can no longer wonder and stand rapt
in awe, is as good as dead.

—Albert Einstein[7]

We have defined the high states of consciousness as the states in which we feel good. Therefore, we shall consider the highest states of consciousness to be those in which good feeling appears in its most intense form.

In the literature of every age and every culture there are writings which describe, in terms of firsthand experience, episodes of extreme joy. These writings differ from one another in many ways: the episodes of intense pleasure take place in different surroundings, are described in different metaphors, and are associated with different religious systems or with no religious system at all. But these accounts of ecstasy have enough in common so that they have come to be recognized by scholars as constituting a distinct body of literature, and as referring to a distinct category of human experience.[82] It is this category of experience, sometimes referred to as "mystical" or "transcendent" experience, which fits our definition in terms of good feeling, and which we shall therefore take as representing the highest state of human consciousness. In these states of mind, joy and love merge into a serene ecstasy that embraces all of creation and is enfolded in it so that life does indeed emit "a fragrance like that of flowers and sweet-scented herbs." This is good feeling in the most intense form, not muddied by the conflicts and dualities of daily existence but distilled and crystal-clear.

As the terms "mystical" and "transcendent" imply, this special

---

[7] As quoted by Lincoln Barnett in *The Universe and Dr. Einstein* (Signet Science Library, 1952), p. 108.

[8] William James, *The Varieties of Religious Experience* (Mentor/New American Library, 1958); Charles Tart, ed., *Altered States of Consciousness* (Wiley, 1969); John White, ed., *The Highest State of Consciousness* (Doubleday/Anchor, 1972); Roland Fischer, "A Cartography of Inner Space," in *Hallucinations: Behavior, Experience, and Theory,* Ronald Siegel and Louis West, eds. (Wiley, 1975).

category of human experience differs from our ordinary experience not merely in intensity of good feeling, but in other respects as well. In the highest states of consciousness, changes occur which are, by the standards of ordinary experience, mysterious indeed. These are not changes that could be detected by watching someone who is in a high state of consciousness: they are changes in the way the world is perceived by a person in that state. The most striking change is a profound sense of unity, a sense that all things are more than interrelated: they are all one thing. In the words of W. T. Stace, "The whole multiplicity of things which comprise the universe are identical with one another and therefore constitute only one thing, a pure unity. The Unity, the One, is the central experience and the central concept of all mysticism."[9] Just as the different facets of a jewel are two-dimensional aspects of a single three-dimensional form, so the various objects and events that we experience seem (in the transcendent state) to be different three-dimensional aspects of a reality that has more dimensions than three.

The sense of unity is especially marked as it applies to the perception of people. There is a deep sense of kinship with one's fellow creatures, a feeling that we are all merely different manifestations, different expressions, different personifications, of one all-encompassing entity. The result is an emotion of universal love and compassion that is an important element in the good feeling of transcendent consciousness. One is directly aware of being part of the human family and of a universal plan and purpose, and this awareness is deeply comforting.

The pervasive feeling of oneness extends even to the distinction between perceiver and perceived, so that the two are felt to be one. There is a loss of the usual sense of self as separate and isolated, a feeling that there is not, and could never be, anything "other" or "alien" from oneself. The world at large, being fully identified with oneself, takes on one's own qualities of life and consciousness, so that the entire universe is sensed as pulsing and aware, alive in every atom.

Not surprisingly, these intense emotions of joy, love, compassion often give rise to the feeling that the experience is a sacred event, a period of being close to divinity or in touch with a higher reality than that of daily existence. Whatever each individual regards as worthy of reverence tends to be reached and evoked during an episode of higher consciousness.

The sense of unity extends also to the perception of time. Instead of perceiving a succession of different moments, a person in this state perceives all moments as being, in a sense, identical, and

---

[9] W. T. Stace, *Mysticism and Philosophy* (J. B. Lippincott Co., 1960), p. 66.

therefore as comprising one eternal moment. Time no longer flows or passes, but seems to stand still. Events still occur in sequence, but they do not seem to take place "in time." The effect of this stoppage of time is a marked sensation of peace and stability. There seems plenty of time for everything, no longer any need to rush from one task to the next. Paradoxically, however, time is perceived as priceless beyond measure; each moment is savored as an opportunity that will never recur. Guilt (which is linked with the past) and anxiety (which is linked with the future) are both absent, because past and future are seen to be illusion. In short, the stoppage of time is not separate from the intense good feeling of transcendent experience, but is an integral part of that feeling-another aspect of an experience that is, above all, unitary.

Space, like time, is often transcended in these highest states of consciousness. When all things are perceived as one thing, all places seem to be one place, and the idea of different places (which is the idea of three-dimensional space) is perceived as illusion.

These are paradoxical experiences; and in fact paradoxes are highly characteristic of transcendent consciousness. Walter Pahnke describes the mystical experience thus: "There is a loss of empirical content in an empty unity which is at the same time full and complete. This loss includes the loss of the sense of self and dissolution of individuality, yet something individual remains to experience the unity. The 'I' both exists and does not exist. The One or Universal Self is both impersonal and personal, both active and inactive."[10]

Paradoxicality, as a general attribute of mystical experience, can be interpreted as a result of the many paradoxical perceptions (such as the stoppage of time) that occur at the higher levels of consciousness; but the *acceptance* of paradoxes is more difficult to account for. This phenomenon—the simultaneous acceptance of mutually contradictory views—can be found among the devout followers of any religious tradition. Many Christians believe, for example, that Jesus Christ is the only begotten son of God; they also believe that we are all God's children. The shift to a higher level of consciousness seems to entail an expansion of consciousness, so that there is room enough for beliefs which might otherwise conflict with one another. Walt Whitman (himself a mystic) wrote:

> Do I contradict myself?
> Very well then I contradict myself.
> (I am large, I contain multitudes.)

---

[10] Walter Pahnke, "Drugs and Mysticism: An Analysis of the Relationship between Psychedelic Drugs and Mystical Consciousness" (Ph.D. dissertation, Harvard University, 1963), p. 70.

Another important characteristic of higher consciousness is what William James called the "noetic" quality of the experience—the absolute inner conviction and certainty that mystical perceptions reveal a higher order of truth than our ordinary experience—revealing, in fact, what is "really there" in the physical, material universe. This feeling is so strong, and so widely reported, that many scholars consider it an important identifying characteristic of mystical experience. To the mystic, our everyday perceptions are illusion; it is only in the states of transcendent consciousness that we are granted a glimpse of reality.

From the point of view of our ordinary consciousness, the altered perceptions of transcendent experience seem to be distortions and misperceptions, and, indeed, they are often referred to as illusions or hallucinations. But to the person experiencing an altered state of consciousness, this different way of looking at the world seems more valid than our usual way of interpreting what we see; it seems to be firmly grounded in knowledge and understanding. In the words of William James, "Mystical states seem to those who experience them to be also states of knowledge. They are states of insight into depths of truth unplumbed by the discursive intellect."[11]

Nor does a person in a transcendent state of consciousness suffer any disability or impairment associated with the altered perceptions. The mystic who reports that "all is one" suffers no inability to distinguish among different objects or among events that occur in succession. Such a report is merely an effort to convey an insight more penetrating than our usual understanding of the nature of space and time.

Thus, far from representing any malfunction or distortion, the perceptions that accompany transcendent consciousness represent a significant enhancement of perceptual skill and capacity, for a person in this condition perceives not only the differences among things but also the essential unity that underlies those differences. Indeed, the terms "illusion" and "hallucination" seem more applicable to our ordinary perceptions than to transcendent perception.

There is no abrupt discontinuity between our normal states of consciousness and the mystical states. Intermediate levels are common. Seeing a beautiful sunset or being with someone we like may not produce complete transcendence but is likely to produce perceptual changes similar in kind (but not degree) to those of mystical transcendence. (The most noticeable of these changes is the altered perception of time. As Albert Einstein said, "When you sit with a nice girl for two hours, it seems like five minutes; but when you sit on a hot

---

[11] James, *Varieties*, p. 293.

stove for five minutes, it seems like two hours. That's relativity.")[12]

      If we think of all the states of human consciousness as lying on a single scale, from the lowest to the highest, then we have a scale of affect or emotional tone that ranges from abject despair to the bliss of transcendence. The midpoint of this scale corresponds to neutral feeling (i.e., an emotional tone that is neither positive nor negative); the upper portion of the scale, from neutral feeling through transcendent bliss, may be thought of as a *scale of higher consciousness.*

      In the next chapter, we shall develop another scale—namely, a scale of dimensional levels. We shall then be in a position to compare the two scales, and in that way to reveal a fundamental relationship between the higher levels of human consciousness and the higher dimensional levels of the world around us.

---

[12] As quoted by Gae Gaer Luce in *Body Time* (Bantam, 1971), p. 14.

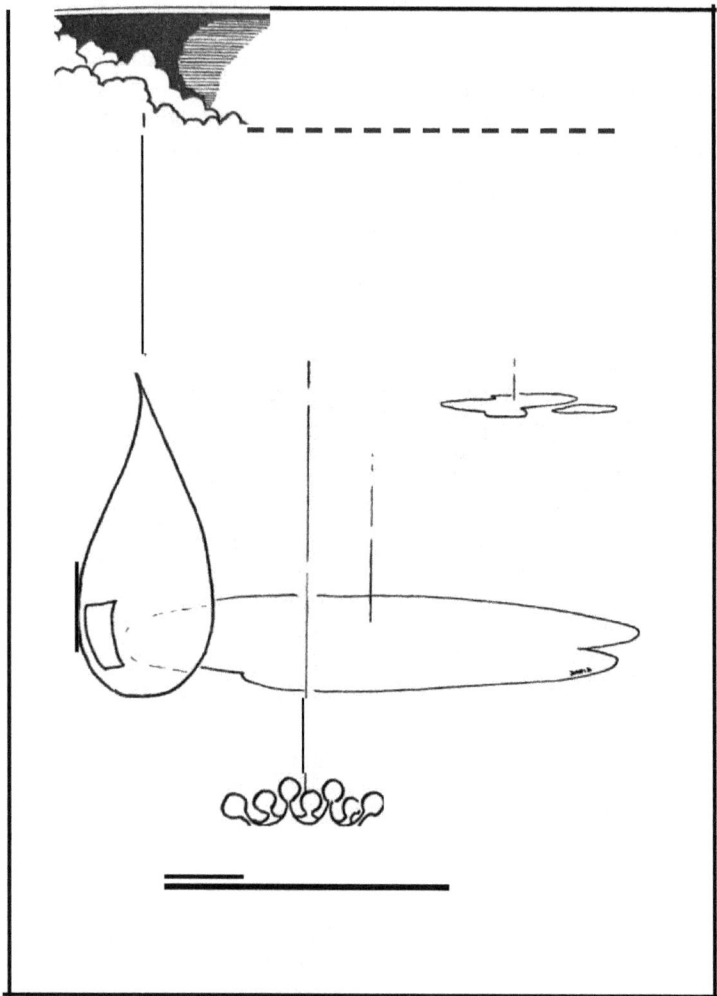

Chapter 4

The Dimensional Level of Human Perception

*It is only in appearance that time is a river. It is
rather a vast landscape and it is the eye of the
beholder that moves.*

—Thornton Wilder
The Eighth Day

Higher consciousness has to do with joy and love and transcendence, and therefore seems quite unrelated to the world of solid objects and plain facts. In this chapter, we shall. take the first steps toward showing that these two categories of experience, the world of spirit and the world of matter, are merely two different aspects—or, to put it more accurately, two different *levels*—of the same reality. The concept that will serve as a unifying link between the two realms is the common idea of *dimensions*. Let us begin, then, by examining the way we perceive the dimensions of the physical world. (In this discussion, we shall use "perceive" in its narrow sense, as referring to "sensory" perception—the receiving of information through our organs of sense.)

We ordinarily think of ourselves as existing in a world of three dimensions. That is, we think of our bodies and the objects around us as having three dimensions and occupying a three-dimensional space. These three dimensions have in common extension in space. The fourth dimension of any object is the dimension that has extension in time.

Consider, for example, a raindrop that forms in a cloud, falls toward Earth for a few minutes, then strikes the ground, splatters, and soaks into the soil, thus ceasing to exist as a raindrop. The three-dimensional *form* of a raindrop is the form that it has at any moment during its existence. The four-dimensional *figure* of the raindrop is the sum of all the three-dimensional forms. Just as any one three-dimensional form represents the existence of the raindrop at one moment, so the four-dimensional figure of the raindrop represents its entire existence, from its creation to its dissolution.

For a clearer idea of the relation between three-dimensional form and four-dimensional figure, let us try to picture the series of three-dimensional forms that the raindrop has during its brief existence. Some of these forms may be similar or even identical to one another, and some not; but let us imagine them all in sequence, each one representing a moment in the life of the raindrop. Now let us combine all these three-dimensional farms in such a way that they coalesce into a single composite figure, stretched out in time, with their original order preserved. This is the four-dimensional figure of the raindrop: it contains the entire existence of the raindrop, from beginning to end.

The raindrop, or any object, exists simultaneously in both modes: as a series of three-dimensional forms and as—our single four-dimensional figure. Three-dimensional form and four-dimensional figure are not two different modes of existence. They are two different aspects of the same existence, and they correspond to two different ways of looking at the same thing: moment by moment, or all at once. In other words, what determines the apparent dimensionality of the world is not any property of the world itself, but how we look at it—our "dimensional mode of perception."

In order to gain a clearer understanding of this idea of different modes of perception that correspond to different dimensional levels, let us imagine an observer in a moving vehicle who looks out at the passing scene through a window. The observer in the moving vehicle is us, and the passing scene represents the four-dimensional universe—i.e., the universe of four-dimensional figures. The window represents a *time window* through which we view the four-dimensional universe. The width of the time window (measured in units of time) determines our mode of perception. Suppose, for example, that the time window is infinitely wide: this would enable the observer in the moving vehicle to see the entire landscape all at once; and, by analogy, it would enable us to perceive the entire four-dimensional universe, from eternal past to eternal future, all at once. Thus, a time window of infinite width corresponds to the four-dimensional mode of perception. A time window with a width of, say, one year would therefore correspond to a dimensional level of less than four.

If we consider the effect of progressively narrower time windows, we find that, as long as the time window has any width at all, the mode of perception is above the three-dimensional level. This is because the time window controls the amount of four-dimensional figure that is seen at one time, and as long as any four-dimensionality enters into the perception, the dimensional level is higher than three. We may conclude, then, that as the width of the time window varies between zero and infinity, the mode of perception varies between three and four dimensions.

We described the effect of a time window of infinite width by saying that it allowed the perception of the entire four-dimensional figure of the universe all at once. Similarly, a time window with a width of one year would enable us to perceive the events of a year all at once. A time window with a width of one hour would enable us to perceive the events of one hour all at once, and so on.

To measure the width of the human time window, then, it is

23

only necessary to determine the interval of time over which we perceive events as happening all at once. To simplify the experimental procedure, we need use only two events—say, two flashes of light, or two sounds. With appropriate instrumentation, we present these two stimuli to an observer in rapid succession, and we reduce the interval between them until the observer can no longer tell them apart (or tell which came first). It seems intuitively reasonable that the observer can easily distinguish between two sounds (or two flashes of light) that are separated by one second, but not between two sounds (or flashes of light) that are separated by only a thousandth of a second. So the width of the human time window must be between a thousandth of a second and one second.

The term "moment" is often used to refer to the "unit" of time in this sense—i.e., the longest interval of time over which successive events seem to be simultaneous. Experimental psychologists have measured the duration of the "moment" for human observers under a variety of conditions and have obtained values ranging from five hundredths of a second to two tenths of a second. J.M. Stroud, after reviewing many of these experiments, concluded that the best estimate of the moment for a human observer is approximately one tenth of a second.[13] This value does not vary appreciably from one individual to another or in the same individual from time to time. Since the exact value is not of crucial importance for our purposes, and since Stroud's estimate is intuitively acceptable and has a solid experimental basis, we may take that value—one tenth of a second—as a working estimate of the width of the human time window.

We may better appreciate the significance of this datum if we try to imagine what perception might be like for beings with a time window, measuring say, ten seconds wide—one hundred times wider than ours. For such beings, a "moment" would be ten seconds long. The sun would appear to move across the sky one hundred times faster than it does for us and one hundred of our days would seem like one day.

In the Book of Psalms (90:4), it is said that "a thousand years in thy sight are but as yesterday, or as a watch in the night." Taking a "watch in the night" as four hours (an ancient tradition), this poetic description implies a time window wider than the human sensory time window by a factor of 2,190,000 (the ratio between a thousand years and four hours). The passage therefore suggests that the deity (Yahweh) addressed by the Psalmist has a time window of approximately two and one-half days.

---

[13] J. M. Stroud, "The Fine Structure of Psychological Time," in *Information Theory in Psychology*, H. Quastler, ed. (Free Press, 1955), pp 147-207.

Another example of a being with a wide time window may be found in the *Bhagavad Gita*, a Hindu religious text, where it is said that 8,640,000,000 years constitute "one day and night of Brahma." This works out to a time window of 10,000 years.

The finding that the human time window has a width of one tenth of a second implies that our mode of perception is between three and four dimensions. But what does it mean to speak of a dimensional level between three and four? We can visualize a three-dimensional form, and we can acquire some conception of a four-dimensional figure; but what visualization corresponds to an intermediate dimensional level?

The visualization that is appropriate to a dimensional level between three and four is that of a *time segment* of a four-dimensional figure. When we look at an object, we do not see its three-dimensional form. Rather, we see a tenth-of-a-second time segment of a four-dimensional figure. (Or, to put it another way, we see the sum of all the instantaneous three-dimensional forms that occupy a time interval of one tenth of a second.)

In constructing the four-dimensional figure of the raindrop, we spoke of combining a series of three-dimensional forms; and, indeed, it is reasonable to think of three-dimensional forms as the elementary components of a four-dimensional figure. But in fact it was tenth-of-a-second time segments, and not three-dimensional forms, that we visualized and combined in that imaginative construction. We visualized tenth-of-a-second time segments because that is the form in which a raindrop (or anything else) is presented to us by our senses, so that is the form in which we naturally tend to visualize things. What we generally refer to as an "object" is not a three-dimensional form but a tenth-of-a-second time segment of a four-dimensional figure.

In dealing with this idea of an object as a time segment, it is important to keep in mind that we do not see time segments in succession. Rather, as in the metaphor of the observer looking out through the window of a moving vehicle, we see a time segment of fixed width (namely, one tenth of a second) moving continuously along the four-dimensional figure of the universe.

The misconception that we see objects as three-dimensional forms is a persistent one, deeply ingrained in our habits of thought. For that reason, it may be worthwhile to emphasize that three-dimensional perception is absolutely impossible. The metaphor of the time window provides one demonstration of this fact: three dimensional perception would correspond to a time window of zero width, and would therefore represent no perception at all. But the same conclusion can also be reached without reference to the time window. An object seen as having only three dimensions, since it would have no extension in the fourth dimension, would have no extension in time—i.e., no duration. An object with no duration would not exist for us.

The impossibility of pure three-dimensional perception can also be seen by considering the fact that our organs of perception have certain built-in delays. Three-dimensional perception would be instantaneous perception, and human physiological mechanisms are not capable of functioning instantaneously. To say that our time window has a width of one tenth of a second is merely a convenient way of specifying the time required for the processing of information by our sense organs and brains.

The number that specifies the width of the time window for human perception—one tenth of a second—is a *dimensional* specification. It specifies the amount of four-dimensionality that is present to all our perceptions. It names a point on the dimensional scale between three and four. It is in units of time because the fourth dimension appears to us in the guise of time. No other units of measurement would be appropriate.

This point on the dimensional scale (specifically, one tenth of a second above "three" on that scale) may be thought of as the "sensory" level because it is associated with sensory perception and its value is determined by the properties of our sensory apparatus—our sense organs and brains. Since we are attempting to establish a correspondence between dimensional levels and levels of consciousness, let us turn now to the "scale of higher consciousness" that was developed in the preceding chapter. If we try to find a place on that scale for sensory impressions, we discover that sensory impressions (being quite independent of good feeling and bad feeling) correspond precisely to the point of neutral feeling that is the lower limit of the scale of higher consciousness.

We now have a point in common between the scale of dimensions and the scale of higher consciousness. The point that is one tenth of a second above "three" on the scale of dimensions corresponds to the lower limit—the "zero point"—on the scale of higher consciousness.

The next step will be to try to establish another point in common between the two scales. For this purpose, we shall compare the four-dimensional mode of perception with transcendent consciousness. However, before we proceed with that comparison, we shall discuss dimensions higher·than the fourth. There are two reasons for this digression into the fifth and sixth dimensions. First, an examination of the relationships among the higher levels of the dimensional scale will enhance our understanding of the principle of dimensional levels. Second, we must deal with an inconsistency that is present in the idea of a four-dimensional universe. This inconsistency has to do with the problem of free will.

Chapter 5

The Fifth and Sixth Dimensions

"Now, there's a real problem for me as I'm trying to tell you this, because all the words I know are three-dimensional. As I was going through this, I kept thinking, 'Well, when I was taking geometry, they always told me there were only three dimensions, and I always accepted that. But they were wrong. There are more.' And, of course, our world, the one we're living in now, is three-dimensional, but the next one definitely isn't. And that's why it's so hard to tell you this. I have to describe it to you in words that are three-dimensional."

—Account of a near-death experience, as reported by
Raymond Moody in *Life After Life*[14]

Change, as we experience it, is change in three dimensions, a shift from one set of three-dimensional forms to the next. Such change is possible only *over time*—i.e., only with the addition of a fourth dimension.

In the same way, four-dimensional change is not possible except by the addition of a fifth dimension. Therefore, if we assume that the universe has only four dimensions, we assume the absence of four-dimensional change. Let us examine this assumption. What does the presence or absence of four-dimensional change mean in terms of our experience?

The four-dimensional figure of the universe is the universe as it exists over all time, from eternal past to eternal future. To say that this four-dimensional figure cannot change is to say that the future—our future—cannot change. No act of will or conscious decision on our part can change it, because we are a part of that four-dimensional universe, and our actions and decisions, like all other events in that universe, are fully predetermined. Thus, a universe of only four dimensions would be a dull place. There would be no room in it for conscious decisions or acts of free will or creativity.

The world-view of modern science, which is based on the assumption that the universe we live in has only four dimensions, embodies the conclusions which follow from that assumption—

---

[14] Raymond Moody, *Life after Live* (Bantam, 1976), p. 26.

namely, that future events are fully determined, and that nothing we do can alter the future in any way (for our actions too are predetermined). Thus, Lincoln Barnett, in *The Universe and Dr. Einstein,* asserts that "the universe, the objective world of reality"—i.e., the four-dimensional universe—"does not 'happen'—it simply exists."[15] A similar idea is expressed by the French physicist Louis de Broglie (in this passage, "space-time" refers to the four-dimensional universe): "Each observer, as time passes, discovers, so to speak, new slices of space-time which appear as successive aspects of the material world, though in reality the ensemble of events constituting space-time exist prior to our knowledge of them."[16]

But most people, arguing only from their experience of living in the world, would disagree with that scientific view. Most of us have a strong intuitive feeling that we can and do affect future events by our conscious decisions and choices—i.e., by our acts of will. For most of us, "free will" is synonymous with "consciousness." To say that a person is fully conscious seems to imply conscious action as well as conscious perception. A world without free will would be a world without creativity. As William Golding puts it, "Free will cannot be debated but only experienced, like a colour or the taste of potatoes."[17]

The deterministic view of modern physics is not based on any realistic consideration of the broad philosophic problem of free will. It is based on the finding that the phenomena that physics tries to explain can be explained satisfactorily with only four dimensions. Physicists then conclude that the universe has no more than four dimensions; and from that conclusion they deduce the principle of determinacy. But there is no real evidence, in the findings of modern physics or anywhere else, that the universe has no more than four dimensions. Let us therefore try to visualize a fifth dimension and see how it allows for the operation of free will.

The first step in visualizing the fifth dimension is to make a dot with a pencil on a piece of paper. After the dot has remained for ten seconds, it should be erased. We may then construct, in retrospect, the four-dimensional figure of that dot which no longer exists. To do this, we follow the same procedure we used with the raindrop. We begin by imagining the dot as it appeared when we first made it, then a moment later, then a moment after that, and so on for ten seconds. (All these appearances are, of course, identical.) Finally, we allow this series of identical dots to coalesce into a single composite figure, spread out in

---

[15] Barnett, *Universe*, p. 72.

[16] Louis de Broglie, "The Scientific Work of Albert Einstein," in *Albert Einstein: Philosopher-Scientist*, P. A. Schilpp, ed. (Harper, 1959), p. 114.

[17] William Golding, *Free Fall* (Pocket Books, 1967), p. 2.

time. This composite figure is the four-dimensional figure of the dot. Its three spatial dimensions are very small; but its fourth dimension has a specific length—namely, ten seconds. Since it has only one significant dimension, we may think of it as a "time line" ten seconds long.

Just as we might imagine an ordinary one-dimensional line expanding into a two-dimensional surface, let us imagine the time line (which is the four-dimensional figure of the dot) expanding into a *time surface.* This time surface is the five-dimensional figure of the dot.

Whereas the four-dimensional figure of the dot consists of a single time line, the five-dimensional figure of the dot (the time surface) contains many time lines—i.e., many four-dimensional figures. Each of these four-dimensional figures represents a single sequence of events, a specific "fate" for the dot, a definite "future." The five-dimensional figure therefore contains many sequences of events—many different "fates" for the dot, many different "futures." In some of these sequences, for instance, the dot might not be erased at the end of ten seconds, or might not be erased at all.

This simple example shows the essential difference between a four-dimensional figure and a five-dimensional figure. A four-dimensional figure contains only one sequence of events, only one past and future, only one possible outcome. A five-dimensional figure, on the other hand, contains many sequences of events, many pasts and futures, many possible outcomes.

The same distinction holds between a four-dimensional universe and a five-dimensional universe. The former contains only one sequence of events, one possible outcome, for every object and for the entire universe. The latter contains many parallel sequences of events, many possible outcomes, for every object and for the entire universe. Change is now possible in the four-dimensional universe that we experience; that is, the future is no longer completely predictable. By postulating that the universe has a fifth dimension, we obtain manifold parallel sequences of events which allow for the operation of free will.

Whereas the four-dimensional figure of a person contains all the experiences of a lifetime, the five-dimensional figure of a person contains all the *possible* experiences of a lifetime, including both those which actually come to be experienced and those not experienced. Clearly, the potential for experience changes during one's lifetime, depending on many factors; in other words, one's five-dimensional figure changes. To allow for change in the five-dimensional figure, we must postulate a sixth dimension.

To visualize the six-dimensional figure of the dot, we simply allow the five-dimensional time surface to expand into a time solid.

In the five-dimensional figure of the dot, all the time lines were on one time surface. But in the six-dimensional figure we can

32

distinguish between two kinds of time lines—those which are confined to a single time surface, and those which move out of the surface to different levels within the time solid. Let us now try to understand the significance of this new dimension of change in terms of human actions and decisions.

In the six-dimensional universe, the four-dimensional figure of a person still contains all the forms, events, and experiences of a lifetime, and the five-dimensional figure of the person still contains as many possibilities as it did in the five-dimensional universe. But, with six dimensions, we are free to move out of the five-dimensional figure formed by our past actions (our personal history), and to move to an entirely new category of perception and experience. In a six-dimensional universe, conditions of existence radically different from anything previously envisioned are possible, regardless of one's present level of consciousness. In other words, with six dimensions—and only with six dimensions—can conscious spiritual evolution, and the inner transformation that comes with the attainment of higher consciousness, take place.

The parables quoted in chapter 2 provide a powerful and accurate metaphor for the type of conscious decision that is possible only in a six-dimensional universe. The discovery of the treasure, or the pearl, represents the discovery of one's innate potential for moving to a new level of consciousness, a mode of being not previously recognized as a realistic possibility.

We can now appreciate the significance of the six-pointed star as an esoteric symbol: it represents the kind of transmutation of the self that is possible only in a universe of six dimensions. It stands for the work done to achieve higher consciousness.

We are also in a position now to appreciate why it has been necessary to discuss the fifth and sixth dimensions here. This book is addressed to readers who are capable of making conscious decisions regarding the attainment of a higher level of consciousness. In a universe of only four dimensions, the system of ideas presented here would be nothing more than an intellectual recreation, a dimensional parlor game. The whole point of this book is to describe a form of conscious activity that is possible only in a six-dimensional universe.

The fifth and sixth dimensions—and, in fact, all dimensional levels higher than that of sensory perception—are real (for us) only in the sense that they are real possibilities. Our senses allow us only a partial view (specifically, a tenth-of-a-second time segment) of the four-dimensional aspect of the universe, and no view at all of dimensional levels higher than the fourth. The fifth and sixth dimensions constitute the (for us) unmanifest portion of the universe.

Our common-sense idea of free will must suffer only one minor

33

blow. We ordinarily feel that our conscious decisions and actions cause some events to happen and others not to happen. But in a six-dimensional universe many events "happen" in that sense. Many are "actualized," including both those which we experience and those which we do not experience. It is this multitude of possibilities actualized in each moment that give the fifth and sixth dimensions their reality. Without those infinite actualizations, the idea of dimensions higher than the fourth makes no sense.

An act of will is therefore not a decision to actualize one or another sequence of events. It is a creative act only in the more limited sense of being a decision to follow one of many sequences, i.e., one of many four-dimensional "time lines." Of the sequences not chosen, some will achieve varying degrees of actualization.

We have so far visualized the six-dimensional universe only in terms of the greatly oversimplified metaphor of the time solid. The following passage, by Peter Ouspensky, provides a more complete and graphic description of the unmanifest reality in which we live:

> If we try to imagine the actualization of all the possibilities of the present moment, then of the next moment, and so on, we shall feel the world growing infinitely, incessantly multiplying by itself and becoming immeasurably rich and utterly unlike the flat and limited world we have pictured to ourselves up to this moment. Having imagined this infinite variety we shall feel a "taste" of infinity for a moment and shall understand how inadequate and impossible it is to approach the problem of time with earthly measures. We shall understand what an infinite richness of time going in all directions is necessary for the actualization of all the possibilities that arise in each moment. And we shall understand that the very idea of arising and disappearing possibilities is created by the human mind, because otherwise it would burst and perish from a single contact with the infinite actualization.[18]

We are now ready to return to the comparison between four-dimensional perception and transcendent consciousness. But from now on, when we refer to the fourth dimension, we shall have in mind a fourth dimension which is contained within higher dimensions, and which therefore allows for the action of conscious beings exercising their free will.

---

[18] Peter Ouspensky, *A New Model of the Universe* (Vintage, 1971), p. 124.

Chapter 6

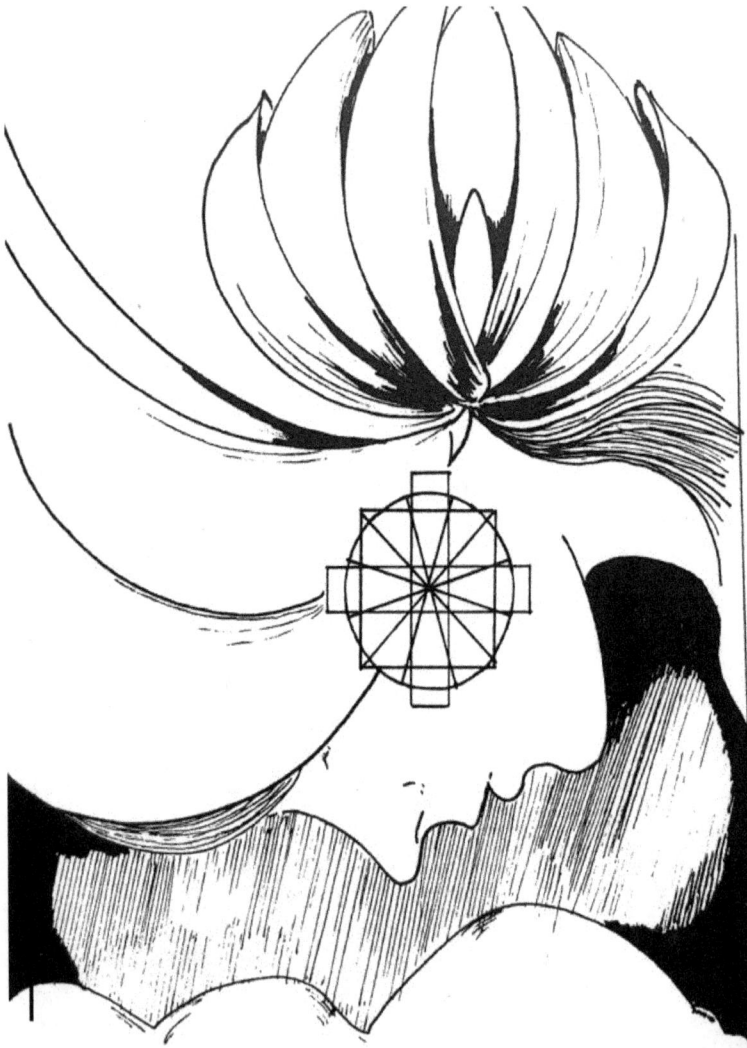

Four-Dimensional and Transcendent Consciousness

All things by immortal power
Near or Far
Hiddenly
To each other linked are
That thou canst not stir a flower
Without troubling of a star

—Francis Thompson,
"The Mistress of Vision"

When we constructed the four-dimensional figure of the raindrop, we arbitrarily chose a particular moment as the starting-point—namely, the moment when the raindrop formed in a cloud. Our choice of a fixed endpoint for the figure—the moment when the raindrop dissolved into the soil—was equally arbitrary. These arbitrary choices had no basis in reality; they had to do only with the word "raindrop." In the real world, as it exists apart from the names we give to things, the "life" of the raindrop is not a separate event, but an integral part of a continuous process. In reality, therefore, the four-dimensional figure of a raindrop, or of anything else, must extend indefinitely far into the past and into the future. In the four-dimensional world, there are no abrupt discontinuities in time where one thing leaves off and something else begins.

A similar line of reasoning applies to the *spatial* characteristics of four-dimensional figures. Thus, the figure of the raindrop, since it includes the droplets that came together to form the raindrop, must also include the cloud in which it formed—for without the word "raindrop" there is nothing to distinguish those droplets from any others. Similarly, when the raindrop soaked into the soil, it became an integral part of the four-dimensional figure of the soil. In space, as in time, four-dimensional figures have no boundaries. The four-dimensional figure of anything includes, in the final analysis, everything. We arbitrarily carve the four-dimensional universe into separate "objects" and "events" so that we can talk about it; but in the four-dimensional reality nothing is separate from anything else. In short, four-dimensional perception, like transcendent perception, is the perception of all things as one.

As we saw in chapter 3, the perception of all things as one is also a prominent characteristic of high states of consciousness, and the other perceptual changes that occur in the high states—the transcendence of time and space—are direct consequences of the perception of unity. We have therefore a strong link between four-dimensional consciousness and transcendent consciousness, and we have taken the first step toward establishing the identity between them.

When we talk about the states of mystical transcendence, however, we are not talking about a mere "perceptual alteration" that might be of interest primarily to students of perception. We are talking, rather, about the condition of mind that has inspired the most sublime artistic and literary creations of humanity, that has enlightened and elevated the human spirit in every age, and that lies at the root of every religious tradition. We are talking about the experience of pure love, transcendent bliss, and profound universal compassion. Relative to the effect of the mystical-religious state on the individual and on human history, purely perceptual changes are little more than technical details. The real challenge is to establish a connection—a credible link—between the unity of four-dimensional perception and the universal love and bliss of transcendent consciousness.

For this purpose, let us examine the way a four-dimensional observer perceives objects, and the universe as a whole, in relation to himself or herself. If we think of this relationship in terms of the four-dimensional figures of observer and observed, it will be immediately apparent that a four-dimensional observer must perceive himself or herself to be one with whatever is perceived. For a human observer, such a perception implies a loss of the usual sense of self as separate and isolated, and, simultaneously, a feeling that there is not, and could not be, anything "other" or "alien" to oneself. Furthermore, to be fully identified with the universe is to perceive the universe as partaking of one's own qualities of life and consciousness, so that the entire universe is perceived as a pulsing, aware thing, alive in every atom. These perceptions follow directly from the perception of all things as one by a human observer.

We cannot deduce logically that joy and love are characteristic of four-dimensionality, but we might expect that any human being who attains four-dimensional consciousness, and who thereby confronts the four-dimensional reality that the universe is alive and we are one with it, will respond to that reality with emotions of joy and love, because this is good news in its most objective and convincing form.

The similarities between four-dimensional consciousness and transcendent consciousness are too striking to be attributed to chance. These are not two different states of consciousness that happen to have some elements in common. They are the same state of consciousness called by two different names.

The parallel between four-dimensional consciousness and

transcendent consciousness gives us a second point (or region) of correspondence between the scale of dimensions and the scale of higher consciousness. (The first point of correspondence between the two scales, established in chapter 4, is represented by the point one tenth of a second above "three" on the scale of dimensions, and by the zero point—representing neutral feeling or sensory perception—on the scale of higher consciousness.) With two points of correspondence, we are now able to conclude that attaining dimensional levels above the tenth-of-a-second level is identical with attaining higher states of human consciousness. In other words, as we go from our ordinary states of consciousness to a higher level on the scale of consciousness, what changes is the *dimensional* level at which we are aware of ourselves and the world around us.

It is important to keep in mind the distinction between the dimensional level of our *perceptions* (which is fixed at the sensory level on the dimensional scale) and the dimensional level of our *consciousness,* which can vary over a wide range. As we go from our ordinary state of consciousness to a higher level (i.e., to a higher level on the dimensional scale), we continue to perceive, through our senses, the same tenth-of-a-second time segment of whatever we look at. Even in transcendent consciousness, there is no change in the dimensional level of the information we receive from our senses. What changes is our interpretation of that information. For example, the senses continue to tell us that objects are separate from one another; but we become aware that the separateness is an illusion and that a fundamental unity underlies the apparent diversity. Our senses continue to tell us that events are occurring one after another, over time, but we become aware that this "time" is an illusion created by our act of perceiving; therefore, our perception of the sequence of events changes in a subtle but unmistakable way.

In four-dimensional *perception* (a hypothetical condition), one would perceive objects as four-dimensional figures; but in four-dimensional *consciousness* (a real condition: transcendent consciousness) objects are seen in the usual way but are interpreted in such a way that they seem to take on many of the properties of four-dimensional figures. These changed interpretations are associated with the stoppage of time in four-dimensional consciousness. Thus, during an episode of transcendent consciousness, a long period of observation may seem to require "only a moment;" all the changes and interactions that occur during this long period may seem to take place in a single moment and seem therefore to constitute a single time segment, which is more like a four-dimensional figure than is the usual tenth-of-a-second time segment. Another way in which these altered interpretations resemble four-dimensional perceptions is in the fact that

40

change, which is an outgrowth of time, seems absent in four-dimensional consciousness as it is in four-dimensional perception.

The most important implication of the link between dimensional levels and levels of consciousness is that the fundamental dichotomy that underlies all our thinking and all our perceiving—the dichotomy between the world of matter and the world of spirit—is bridged. Matter (as we experience it) is that which has extension in space; it has its place on the dimensional scale. Spirit, the stuff of higher consciousness, is merely a higher level on the same scale. Matter and spirit are not fundamentally different, nor do they in any sense have equal value: they are related as lower and higher orders of dimensionality, with one shading gradually into the other.

Having established a dimensional scale of higher consciousness, we can now speak accurately and scientifically, and not merely in poetic metaphor, of spiritual values and inner development as representing the higher dimensions of human experience. The absence of any mention of higher consciousness in dictionary definitions of "dimension" is an oversight: dimensions have as much to do with transcendence as with solid objects.

Chapter 7

Time and Immortality

The mortal in whose heart the knots of ignorance are untied becomes immortal.

—Katha Upanishad[19]

To understand the relation between time and dimensionality, let us again imagine a person riding in a moving vehicle, looking at the passing scene through a window. This imaginary situation is analogous to the situation of a human observer looking at the four-dimensional universe through a sensory time window. Through the window we see a time segment of fixed width (namely, one-tenth of a second) moving along the four-dimensional figure of the universe. This movement (which is represented in the metaphor by the motion of the vehicle) is the passage of time.

The passage of time, then, is not a property of the four-dimensional universe. Rather, the passage of time results from the manner in which we ordinarily observe the four-dimensional universe. The four-dimensional universe is in fact beyond time, outside the flow of time.

Any four-dimensional figure is similarly outside of time. Consider, for example, the raindrop discussed earlier. From the point of view of ordinary human perception, the raindrop comes into existence, lasts for some period of time, and then ceases to exist. But at the four-dimensional level, these events are permanent properties of the four-dimensional figure. As a four-dimensional figure, the raindrop does not come into existence at some time and cease to exist at some other time: it simply exists, outside of time. Existence at the four-dimensional level is eternal existence. As a four-dimensional figure, the raindrop is immortal.

Since all objects (including our bodies) exist as four-dimensional figures, all objects (including our bodies) are immortal. This kind of immortality—existence outside of time, as a four-dimensional figure—can only be experienced in the four-dimensional (transcendent) mode of consciousness.

Thus, the logic of dimensions leads inescapably to the conclusion that we are immortal—and yet it is common knowledge that no human being lives forever, or even for much more than a century.

---

[19] Upanishads, p. 24

What are we to make of this conflict between the logic of dimensions and the evidence of our senses?

We tend to believe that our views about death are based on conjecture or faith, because most of us have had no direct experience of death. But in fact our views about death are based on direct experience—not of death, but of time. The mystic, for example, has direct experience of the fact that our existence at the higher level—our real existence—is outside of time. Therefore, to the mystic, death is an illusion, immortality the reality. At the other extreme from the mystic is the person who has no experience whatsoever of the higher levels of consciousness and therefore no direct knowledge of existence outside of time. Such a person might well perceive death as the end of individual existence and as representing total annihilation of the personality. This is the materialistic view—the view logically associated with the dimensional level of sensory perception. According to this view, death is the reality, immortality an illusion.

In most people, the level of consciousness varies over time in such a way as to provide occasional glimpses of a mode of existence that is outside of time, but a clear or lasting perception of that condition is rare. Most of us have a view of death that is intermediate between that of the mystic and that of the materialist. For most of us, death seems to be the end of individual bodily existence, but we do not rule out the possibility that some portion of the personality may continue to exist in time following bodily death.

Each of these views about time and immortality has its own internal validity. Each is based on direct sensory experience, and each can be supported by logical arguments ·and empirical evidence. It seems impossible to choose among them, and presumptuous to try; however, the principle of dimensional levels points to a clear choice. According to that principle, the point of view associated with a higher dimensional level of perception and experience is always the more valid point of view. Thus, according to the principle of dimensional levels, the mystic is correct: death is an illusion, and we are all immortal.

But this kind of immortality may not be quite what we have in mind when we think of "eternal life." The kind of immortality that we possess as four-dimensional figures has nothing to do with dying or not dying. It has to do with the fact that the moments of our lives do not vanish into the past but exist eternally in the four-dimensional figure of the universe. Eternal existence is not a condition to be attained at some future date, or by indefinite postponement of bodily death. Eternal existence is present right now, in this moment and every moment.

In Dostoevsky's novel *The Possessed,* Stavrogin asks Kirilov (who has recently had a transcendent experience), "Have you come to believe in a future, eternal life, then?" **"No,"** Kirilov replies, "not in a future, eternal life, but in this present, eternal life. There are moments—you can reach moments—when time suddenly stops and becomes eternal."[20]

These moments when "time suddenly stops" are, of course, episodes of transcendent consciousness. They teach us that immortality is present in every moment of our lives.

A procedure for visualizing one's immortal existence—i.e., one's existence as a four-dimensional figure—was described by the anonymous author of the *Hermetica* in about 200 A.D.: "Think that you are not yet begotten, think that you are in the womb, that you are young, that you are old, that you are dead, that you are in the world beyond the grave, grasp all that in your thought at once, all times and places."[21] This simple meditation, which Maurice Nicoll refers to as the "Hermetic exercise,"[22] is recommended by its author as a way of changing oneself into "eternal substance."

[20] Fyodor Dostoevsky, *The Possessed*, trans. A. R. MacAndrew (Signet, 1962), p. 223.
[21] *Hermetica*, trans. Walter Scott (Oxford University Press, 1924), p. 221.
[22] Maurice Nicoll, *Living Time and the Integration of the Life*, (London: Vincent Stuart, 1952), p. 101.

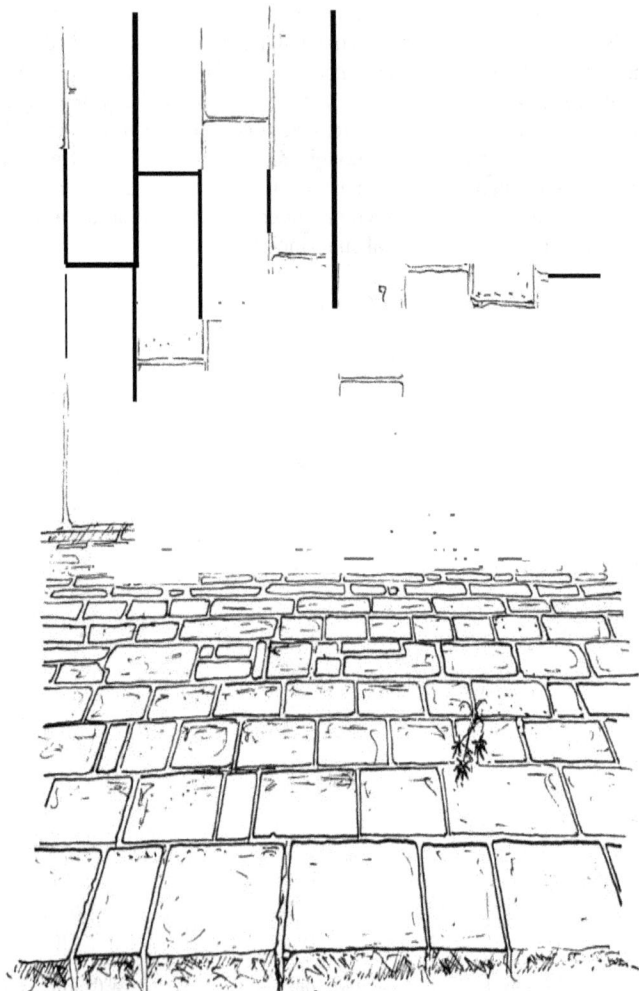

Chapter 8

Faith

But there are earlier and loftier beauties than [those of the realms of sense]. In the sense-bound life we are no longer granted to know them, but the Soul, taking no help from the organs, sees and proclaims them. To the vision of these we must mount, leaving sense on its own low level.

—Plotinus
Ennead I. 6.4.

The word "faith" is used in a variety of ways. We speak of having faith in a person, or faith that it will rain. We also use "faith" to refer to belief in God or in religion. When we refer to the Jewish faith or the Muslim faith, we mean the set of beliefs associated with a particular religious system.

But "faith" also has an esoteric meaning which, even though it has elements in common with the meanings given above, is distinct from them. In its esoteric meaning, "faith" refers to the awareness that there are higher levels of reality than this one, and that these higher levels (which we now know to be higher *dimensional* levels) can be attained by human beings.

This alternative definition is derived from teachings that lie at the core of the Christian tradition. Strangely, even though Jesus himself is quoted in the Gospels as using the word in its esoteric sense, subsequent Christian writers, from ancient times down to the present, have scrupulously avoided the original Christian usage and have used "faith" to mean sectarian belief. The meaning that Jesus gave to the word does not even appear today in most dictionaries of the English language.

Two parables, both taken from the first book of the New Testament, indicate the esoteric sense in which Jesus used the word "faith."

In the first of these stories (Matt. 8:5-13) a centurion—an officer in the Roman army—asks Jesus to heal his servant, who, he says, is "lying paralyzed at home in terrible distress."

Jesus says, "I will come and heal him."

"Lord," says the centurion, "I am not fit to have you come under my roof; but only say the word, and my servant will be healed. For I am a man under authority, with soldiers under me; and I say to one 'Go,' and he goes, and to another, 'Come,' and he comes, and to my slave, 'Do this,' and he does it."

The onlookers must have been somewhat bewildered by this speech. Exactly what do the taking and giving of orders, and the military chain of command, have to do with Jesus going to the soldier's house?

And they must have been even more puzzled when Jesus turned to them and said, "Truly, I say unto you, not even in Israel"—that is, not even among God's chosen people—"have I seen such faith." He then grants the soldier's request, and the servant is healed.

To understand this parable, we must first realize that all the enigmatic parables of the New Testament Gospels refer to spiritual values. Thus, in the words spoken by the centurion, military rank is a metaphor for spiritual "rank"—i.e., level of inner development. The centurion is telling Jesus, in the subtle, indirect way so characteristic of parables, that he (the centurion) understands the concept of levels of spiritual excellence. Having that understanding, he recognizes that Jesus has such spiritual power that he has only to "say the word, and my servant will be healed." And he also knows that Jesus is so far above him in spiritual attainment, so far superior to him as a person, that he, the centurion, is not fit to have Jesus under his roof. This understanding that the centurion has—this comprehension of the idea of different levels of spiritual attainment—is what Jesus calls "faith."

This definition of faith is confirmed and sharpened in the parable of the Canaanite woman (Matt. 15:22-28), who approaches Jesus begging him to have mercy on her. Her daughter, she says, is "severely possessed by a demon." But Jesus will not even speak to her: "he did not answer her a word."

The disciples intervene on her behalf, and Jesus explains to them that he was sent only to "the lost sheep of Israel"—that is, only to his fellow Jews.

The woman now comes and kneels before him, saying, "Lord, help me."

He answers, "It is not fair to take the children's bread and throw it to the dogs."

"Yes, Lord," she says, "yet even the dogs eat the crumbs that fall from their master's table."

What happens next is all the more instructive because it is so unexpected. "O woman," he says, "great is your faith! Be it done for you as you desire." And the daughter is healed instantly.

From this parable there emerges a concept of faith that has been stripped clean of every vestige of "belief." "Faith" here is set in exact opposition to belief. The woman to whom Jesus attributes great faith is a nonbeliever, a heathen, a worshipper of false idols. When he says that he helps only Jews, she does not say, "O Lord, I accept the teachings of Jews."

What finally persuades Jesus that this woman has great faith is her spiritual intelligence, her understanding of transcendent matters, her comprehension of the psychology of the higher states of consciousness. She accepts her role of the dog begging for crumbs, a timeless metaphor for abject humility; but then she shows him that her humility has its origin, not in a low estimate of her own worth, but in a deep spiritual understanding. She shows him that she can recognize holiness when she sees it, and knows enough to humble herself unashamedly before it.

Belief has to do with institutional credos; faith, with the possibilities inherent in the human spirit. One *believes*, let us say, in the doctrine of the remission of sins, or in the efficacy of baptism; but faith is the understanding that these sectarian beliefs and rituals constitute a human effort to forge a link between our material existence and something higher. Faith contains a strong element of stability and focus, a steadiness and singleness of purpose, that is not present in the idea of belief. Belief has to do with this world, and is therefore concerned with the multiplicity of things; but faith represents a turning toward a higher state of being, and partakes of the essential unity of that state.

"Faith" in this sense can have only one object, and seeming differences among religious "faiths" are merely variations in metaphor. It is only in metaphor, and not in substance, that one religious creed differs from another, for they all draw their being and sustenance from what Alan Watts called "that perennial philosophy that is the gold within the sectarian dross of every great religion."[23]

Wordsworth describes spiritual growth as a process in which "persuasion and belief" ripen into faith, which then becomes a "passionate intuition." The first step in this process, the first glimmering of faith, is an awakening to the fact that there are certain beliefs, and a common element in many other beliefs, that are of a different order from the rest, and call for a different psychological attitude.

The maturing of faith is a gradual zeroing-in, a gradual steadying and centering, on the unitary principle of a higher level of being. This "common element" is perceived more clearly and encountered more frequently, and the "different psychological attitude," as it becomes more familiar and natural, is experienced as a growing sense of comprehension and reverence.

We may start out, for example, believing in a particular god and a corresponding set of doctrines; then we may gradually discover that our god is no different from the god of the Bantu and the Eskimo, or

---

[23] Alan Watts, *Behold the Spirit* (Vintage, 1947), p. xi.

from the One of Buddhism. Progressing further, we may discover that the name "god" designates a higher level of being, a higher concept of the meaning of life; it is at this point that we begin to have "faith" in the sense in which Jesus used that word. We go on from there to enlarge our knowledge and understanding of this higher level, and in so doing we enlarge and expand our faith, raising it to progressively higher forms.

In its mature form, faith is the full comprehension that there are higher realities than the world shown to us by our senses, and that—in the words of Plotinus—"to the vision of these we must ascend, leaving sense in its own low place." Mature faith has severed the cord that once connected it with belief, and has moved on to a higher form of comprehension. The green bud of mere credulity has become the resplendent blossom of passionate intuition.

Chapter 9

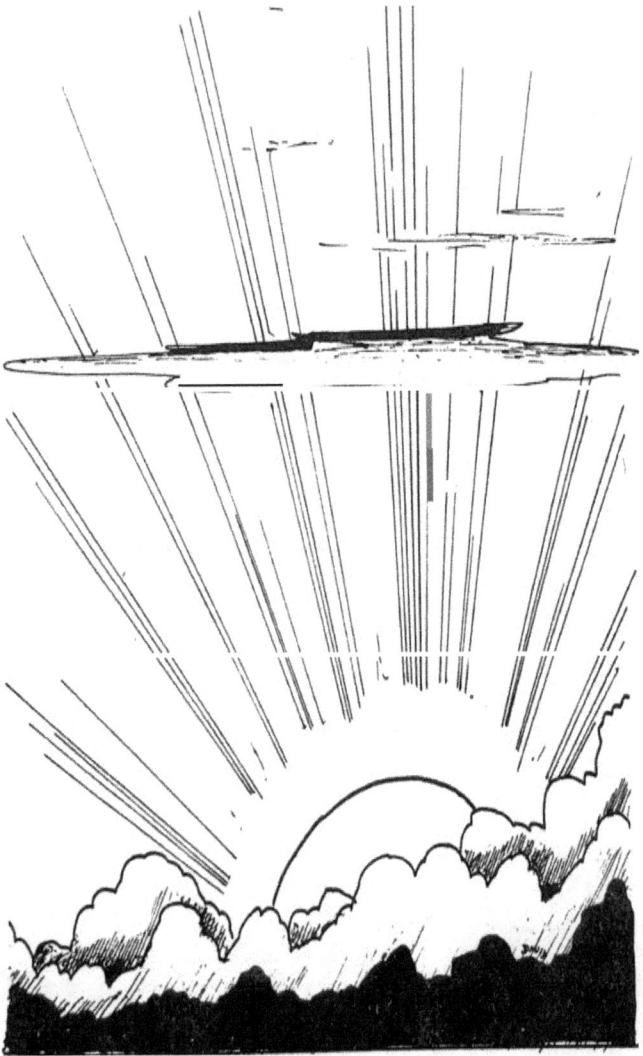

The Beginning

You are already a Buddha: you have only to know the fact.

—Bhagwan Shree Rajneesh,
The Book of the Secrets

Opinions differ widely as to which technique, or which combination of techniques, is most effective and practicable for supplementing the yoga of knowledge; and, of course, the requirements and possibilities vary considerably from one individual to another.[24] In evaluating techniques, it is well to bear in mind that opinions in this field, besides being diverse, are strongly held. There is no substitute for being well- informed concerning a variety of techniques, so that one does not need to rely entirely on the advice of others. Above all, there is no substitute for keeping clearly in mind the nature of the goal, which is the attainment of a higher dimensional level of consciousness. If we keep that goal squarely in front of us during our seeking, the problem of technique will resolve itself.

The very high states of consciousness should be approached with caution. Verbal descriptions cannot adequately convey the degree of strangeness these states may present to someone heretofore immersed in the lower-dimensional reality of ordinary experience. A sudden and unexpected transition from ordinary consciousness to a state of transcendence may produce an abrupt withdrawal of the usual criteria of reality: three-dimensional space, time that passes, the multiplicity of things, the illusion of separateness. One may feel that one's mind is indeed about to "burst and perish from a single contact with the infinite actualization." As if this were not enough, an experience of this type may also involve an abrupt opening of the "subconscious" mind, so that repressed fears and anxieties rise suddenly to the surface of conscious awareness. These kinds of situations may arise, for example, in cases of religious conversion, or through the practice of meditation or the ingestion of psychedelic

---

[24] I recommend the following readings, listed in order of personal preference: Tart, *Altered States*, Chs. 27, 22, 13; Swami Janakananda Saraswati, *Yoga, Tantra & Meditation*, trans. Sheila La Frage (Ballantine, 1976); Alice Christensen and David Rankin, *the Light of Yoga Society Beginner's Manual* (Simon & Schuster, 1972); Bhagwan Shree Rajneesh, *The Book of The Secrets* (Harper/Colphon, 1974); Baba Ram Dass, *Be Here Now* (Crown, 1971).

substances without proper preparation and guidance; they may even happen with no apparent cause.

Though these negative experiences occur in the course of more gradual approaches to higher consciousness, they are less disconcerting when taken a little at a time. There is no need to avoid or reject them. The bliss of higher consciousness both rises above and encompasses those experiences and feelings that we might ordinarily regard as negative. A high state of consciousness that had nothing in it of the negative side of human experience would be like a great symphony with all the bass notes and minor chords left out, or a beautiful painting with all the somber tones removed: though the result might be "pretty," it would be shallow and unimpressive. Viewed from a higher dimensional perspective, such a state of consciousness would appear not merely as lacking "negative" elements, but lacking elements that, negative or not, constitute a major portion of the total human experience.

The primary psychological skill that is required in order to approach the highest states of consciousness is the ability to discover in every negative emotion and perception its positive mirror image, and then to transcend the resulting dichotomy. It is equally necessary to learn the hard lesson that every event and experience that we take to be positive also contains its opposite. One who ventures into these realms of higher consciousness must be prepared to confront terror and despair, to absorb and accept them, to see them as emotions to be cherished simply because they are possible only for living, conscious beings, and then to rise to a level of perception at which these negative feelings, along with their positive counterparts, are viewed from a broader perspective.

The greatest danger presented by these negative aspects of higher consciousness is not that one will become trapped in them or be harmed by the encounter; it is that such an encounter might lead one to abandon the seeking, and thus to fall into a pattern of existence which, however busy and effective it may be in worldly terms, is nevertheless, when viewed from a higher dimensional perspective, without direction.

Before we can improve our relationship to the universe as a whole, we must learn where we stand in relation to it, and realize that the universe as we ordinarily perceive it (as a three-dimensional manifestation) is a negligible portion of the whole. We must become aware that what we see through our narrow time window is only an infinitesimal fraction of all there is, and that the entire universe (including ourselves) has its real existence in the higher dimensions. To comprehend that many-dimensioned reality is beyond our present ability; but we can know that it exists, we can have enough respect for it to learn something about it, and we can try to realize some of its implications for our daily life in time.

We must learn the rules of the divine game before we can begin consciously to play a role in it. And once we have learned them we shall discover that learning *is* the game, and that "success" lies in knowing and understanding—the attainment of wisdom. We need to be able to comprehend—to get our minds around—the awesome, many-dimensioned conception that is the universe of potential human experience. We need to expand our consciousness so that it can contain reality; and once we have expanded our consciousness sufficiently, we shall find new realities, higher still, inviting us to further seeking.

Each of us, like any object of our experience, exists simultaneously as a single four-dimensional figure and as a series of three-dimensional forms; this property is as true of us as it is of the raindrop. Three-dimensional form and four-dimensional figure are not two different modes of existence, but merely different aspects of the same existence. As we exist at the lower-dimensional level, we are separate and distinct from one another. As we exist at the four-dimensional level, we are beyond form and separateness: we are spirit, and we are one.

The level at which we experience ourselves (and which we commonly mistake for "reality") lies, as we have seen, between those two dimensional levels. We know ourselves as flesh and form, but we sometimes sense dimly that our real existence is at a higher level; we conceive ourselves to be separate from one another, but we are vaguely aware of our essential commonality.

The gradual loss of separateness, as we ascend toward the unity of four-dimensional consciousness, corresponds to the loss of "ego" that is a necessary part of inner development. To people who are strongly committed to individual achievement and competition, such a path will seem at times like a surrender of individuality, but in fact the only thing that is surrendered is the bleak isolation of lower-dimensional experience; and that was never anything but illusion. The process is, in fact, a gradual enlargement and enrichment—an "eternalization"—of the individual identity, a broadening of that identity to include the common ground of all being.

Simultaneous existence at all dimensional levels is a property of all objects, including our bodies. This truth is the meaning of the ancient teaching that "you are already a Buddha:" we exist now at any dimensional level to which we may aspire. As Kirilov puts it in *The Possessed,* "Man is unhappy because he doesn't know he's happy. That's the only reason. The man who discovers that will become happy that very minute."

A Buddhist tale tells of a disciple who approached a Zen master asking for the enlightenment that would raise him to a higher level of being.

"Why don't you ask for a horse?" asked the master. "But I already have a horse."

The master was silent.

Notes

CHAPTER 1

1. *Plato Selections*, ed. Raphael Demos (Scribner's, 1927), p. 268. These words are spoken by Socrates, quoting Diotima.
2. For a historical treatment of jnana yoga, see Ernest Wood, *Great Systems of Yoga* (Citadel Press, 1966), pp. 61 ff.

CHAPTER 2

1. *The Upanishads: Breath of the Eternal*, trans. Swami Prabhavananda and Frederick Manchester (Mentor, 1957), p. 48.
2. John Michell, *City of Revelation* (Ballantine, 1973), p. 16.
3. R.A. Schwaller de Lubicz, *The Temple in Man*, trans. R. and D. Lawlor (Autumn Press, 1977), p. 67.
4. Matt. 13:14-66.

CHAPTER 3

1. As quoted by Lincoln Barnett in The Universe and Dr. Einstein (Signet Science Library, 1952), p. 108.
2. William James, *The Varieties of Religious Experience* (Mentor/New American Library, 1958); Charles Tart, ed., *Altered States of Consciousness* (Wiley, 1969); John White, ed., *The Highest State of Consciousness* (Doubleday/Anchor, 1972); Roland Fischer, "A Cartography of Inner Space," in *Hallucinations: Behavior, Experience, and Theory*, Ronald Siegel and Louis West, eds. (Wiley, 1975).
3. W.T. Stace, *Mysticism and Philosophy* (J.B. Lippincott Co., 1960), p. 66.
4. Walter Pahnke, *Drugs and Mysticism: An Analysis of the Relationship between Psychedelic Drugs and Mystical Consciousness* (Ph.D. dissertation, Harvard University, 1963), p. 70.
5. James, *Varieties*; p. 293.
6. As quoted by Gay Gaer Luce in *Body Time* (Bantam, 1971), p. 14.

CHAPTER 4

1. J.M. Stroud, "The Fine Structure of Psychological Time," in *Information Theory in Psychology*, H. Quastler, ed. (Free Press, 1955), pp. 147-207.

CHAPTER 5

1. Raymond Moody, *Life after Life* (Bantam, 1976), p. 26.
2. Barnett, *Universe*, p. 72.
3. Louis de Broglie, "The Scientific Work of Albert Einstein" in *Albert Einstein: Philosopher-Scientist*, P.A. Schilpp, ed. (Harper, 1959), p. 114.
4. William Golding, *Free Fall* (Pocket Books, 1967), p. 2.
5. Peter Ouspensky, *A New Model of the Universe* (Vintage, 1971), p. 124.

CHAPTER 7

1. Upanishads, p. 24.
2. Fyodor Dostoevsky, *The Possessed*, trans. A. R. MacAndrew (Signet, 1962), p. 223.
3. *Hermetica*, trans. Walter Scott (Oxford Univ. Press, 1924), p. 221.
4. Maurice Nicoll, *Living Time and the Integration of the Life*, (London: Vincent Stuart, 1952), p. 101.

CHAPTER 8

1. Alan Watts, *Behold the Spirit* (Vintage, 1947), p. xi.

CHAPTER 9

1. I recommend the following readings, listed in order of personal preference: Tart, *Altered States*, Chs. 27, 22, 13; Swami Janakananda Saraswati, *Yoga, Tantra, & Meditation*, trans. Sheila La Frage (Ballantine, 1976); Alice Christensen and David Rankin, *The Light of Yoga Society Beginner's Manual* (Simon & Schuster, 1972); Bhagwan Shree Rajneesh, *The Book of The Secrets* (Harper/Colphon, 1974); Baba Ram Dass, *Be Here Now* (Crown, 1971).